NFL TODAY

THE STORY OF THE
JACKSONVILLE JAGUARS

NFL TODAY

THE STORY OF THE JACKSONVILLE JAGUARS

GORDON PUESCHNER

CREATIVE EDUCATION

Cover: Jaguars offense, 2008 (top), cornerback
Rashean Mathis (bottom)
Page 2: Quarterback David Garrard
Pages 4–5: 2008 Jacksonville Jaguars
Pages 6–7: Kick returner Brian Witherspoon

....

Published by Creative Education
P.O. Box 227, Mankato, Minnesota 56002
Creative Education is an imprint of
The Creative Company
www.thecreativecompany.us

Design and production by Blue Design
Design Associate: Sarah Yakawonis
Printed in the United States of America

Photographs by Corbis (Charles W. Luzier/Reuters),
Getty Images (Doug Benc, John Biever/Sports
Illustrated, Scott Boehm, Neil Brake/AFP, Paul K.
Buck/AFP, David Drapkin, Stephen Dunn, Bill Frakes/
Sports Illustrated, Larry French, Sam Greenwood,
Otto Greule Jr./Allsport, Wesley Hitt, Simeone
Huber, Allen Kee/NFL, Andy Lyons/Allsport, David
Maxwell/AFP, Al Messerschmidt, Joe Robbins, Eliot
J. Schechter, David Stluka, Robert Sullivan/AFP, Joe
Traver//Time & Life Pictures)

Library of Congress Cataloging-in-Publication Data

Pueschner, Gordon.
The story of the Jacksonville Jaguars / by Gordon
Pueschner.
p. cm. — (NFL today)
Includes index.
ISBN 978-1-58341-759-1
1. Jacksonville Jaguars (Football team)—History—
Juvenile literature. I. Title. II. Series.

GV956.J33P84 2008
796.332'640975912—dc22   2008022690

First Edition
9 8 7 6 5 4 3 2 1

CONTENTS

ON THE SIDELINES

MEET THE JAGUARS

DREAMING BIG

X- -

Jacksonville is valuable to the United States as a whole due to its important role as a shipping port, with all kinds of cargo—including automobiles—being moved on its waters.

The settlement that became Jacksonville, Florida, was founded on the banks of the St. John's River and the Atlantic Ocean in 1791. In 1822, the city was named after General Andrew Jackson, the first military governor of Florida. The city quickly became a distribution hub for sugar and citrus crops, and by the 1900s, the film industry had established more than 30 movie studios there. Later, Jacksonville became known as a center for biomedical technology and diversified manufacturing. But until the 1990s, the city was missing something: a big-league sports franchise. That changed in 1995 when a brand-new National Football League (NFL) team called the Jacksonville Jaguars took the field.

The Jaguars' history began in August 1989 when a group called "Touchdown Jacksonville!"—led by millionaire businessmen Thomas Petway and J. Wayne Weaver—was formed with the goal of bringing an NFL team to this northeastern Florida city. Finally, after years of work to convince league officials that Jacksonville had the resources and fan base to support a team, the group was rewarded. On November 30, 1993, the NFL announced that Jacksonville would receive one of two new expansion franchises.

In February 1994, Tom Coughlin was hired as the Jaguars' first head coach. Coughlin had been an assistant coach for two successful NFL teams—the Green Bay Packers and the New York Giants—and was known as a detailed, no-nonsense coach. As the club began building its first roster, Coughlin was given control over all draft choices and player signings. "I wouldn't have done it any other way," Coughlin said. "These days, it's imperative to have control of your team's direction and personnel."

In February 1995, the NFL held an expansion draft in which the Jaguars and the Carolina Panthers, the league's other new team, were allowed to select some players from the existing 28 NFL franchises. Coach Coughlin chose veteran quarterback Steve Beuerlein and defensive lineman Paul Frase, as well as explosive wide receiver Jimmy Smith. After the expansion draft, Coughlin put together the franchise's first trade. He sent two draft picks to Green Bay for Mark Brunell, a young, left-handed quarterback known for his quick feet.

Coach Coughlin felt that the "heart and soul" of a football team was the offensive line. So, with the team's first

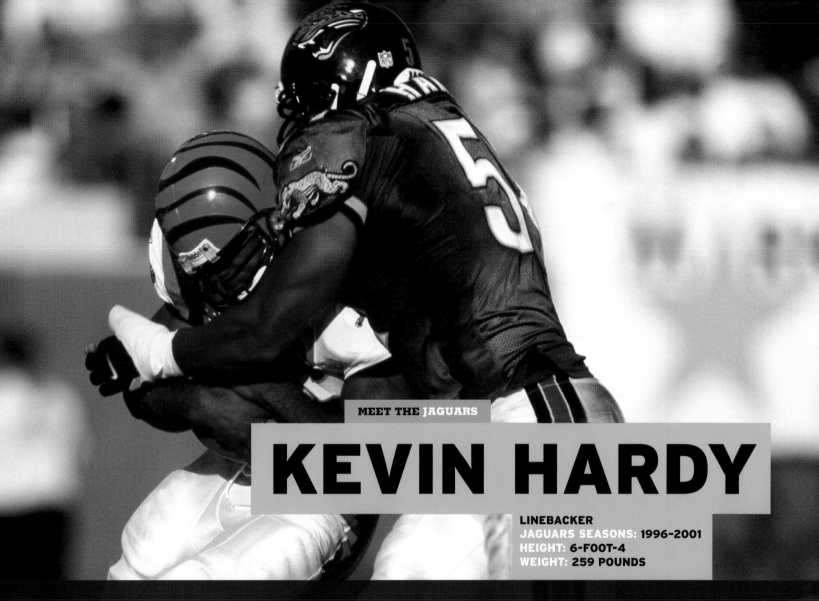

KEVIN HARDY

LINEBACKER
JAGUARS SEASONS: 1996-2001
HEIGHT: 6-FOOT-4
WEIGHT: 259 POUNDS

Kevin Hardy was a fast, bruising linebacker who helped anchor the Jacksonville defense for six seasons. After coming out of the University of Illinois as the second overall choice in the 1996 NFL Draft, Hardy didn't waste any time making a name for himself. In his rookie year, he notched 64 tackles and 5.5 sacks to help carry the Jaguars to their first playoff appearance. "He's been effective on the blitz. He's done everything you could ask of a rookie to do," said defensive end Jeff Lageman. "Rarely do you find a rookie who can step in and make a difference." Over the next few years, Hardy became a one-man wrecking crew, equally adept at blitzing the quarterback and stuffing the run. Hardy sometimes seemed to be everywhere on the field at once. His best season by far was 1999, when he led all AFC linebackers with 10.5 sacks. "As a linebacker, you've got to be involved in every phase of the game," Hardy said, explaining his efforts to be versatile. "It's not just tackles, and it's not just interceptions. It's everything."

TOUCHDOWN JACKSONVILLE!

In 1989, Touchdown Jacksonville! was formed to lure an NFL franchise to Jacksonville. A year later, NFL commissioner Paul Tagliabue announced that the league would expand by two teams for the 1995 season. The group quickly got to work, but the northeastern Florida city was considered a long shot because of its relatively small media market and the fact that two NFL teams, the Tampa Bay Buccaneers and Miami Dolphins, and three major college teams already called Florida home. But that wasn't the only trouble. Touchdown Jacksonville! had financial problems, leading many members of the group to drop out. At one point in 1993, after the Jacksonville city council denied funds for a stadium, the group closed its offices. A month later, however, encouraged by NFL officials, Touchdown Jacksonville! got back in the race. On November 30 of that year, Jacksonville was awarded the NFL's 30th franchise. The next day, a helicopter landed at midfield of Gator Bowl Stadium, which was initially intended to be the home of the new team, and majority owner Wayne Weaver (pictured) stepped onto the field to celebrate with 25,000 cheering fans.

pick in the 1995 NFL Draft, Jacksonville selected offensive tackle Tony Boselli, a former All-American at the University of Southern California. Coughlin liked his strength and character and hoped he would anchor the Jaguars' offensive line for years to come. In addition to Boselli, the Jaguars used a first-round pick to select running back James Stewart from the University of Tennessee.

On September 3, 1995, more than 72,000 fans packed into Jacksonville Municipal Stadium to watch the new team in teal and gold take the field for the first time. The Jaguars lost the game to the Houston Oilers, 10–3, but Jacksonville fans cheered wildly just the same.

In the fifth game of the season, Jacksonville faced the Oilers in Houston's Astrodome, and Brunell stepped in for the struggling Beuerlein in the fourth quarter with Jacksonville down 16–10. Brunell rallied the team, leading the offense down the field and ending the drive with a 15-yard strike to wide receiver Desmond Howard for the win. One week after that, the Jaguars won their first home game. The 20–16 upset over the Pittsburgh Steelers would seem even more special after the season when the Steelers marched all the way to the Super Bowl.

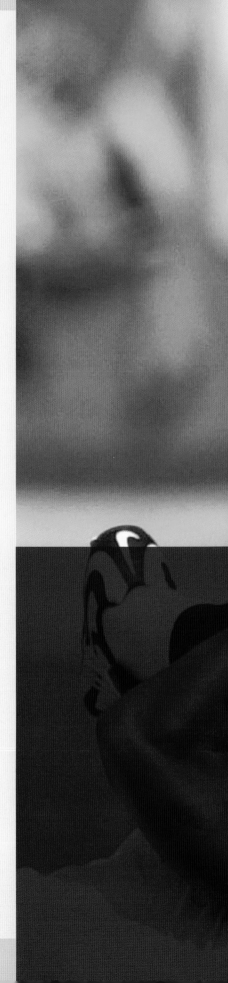

X A 6-foot-7 and 325-pound tackle, Tony Boselli was the team's first-ever draft pick in 1995—in 2006, he would become the first player inducted into the Jaguars' Hall of Fame as well.

Although Jacksonville finished its inaugural season just 4–12, it fought hard every week, losing five games by seven points or fewer. Boselli and tackle Brian DeMarco had anchored a stout offensive line, and Brunell had proven to be one of the American Football Conference's (AFC) most exciting quarterbacks. "I studied players throughout the 1994 season, and I was excited about Mark's athleticism, his toughness, his ability to move in the pocket, and his arm strength," Coughlin said of his quarterback. "I just felt like this would be the guy that we would want to lead our team."

In the months before their second season, the Jaguars continued to add talent. Among the key offensive additions were wide receiver Keenan McCardell. Defensively, the team added bite by bringing in hard-hitting linebacker Kevin Hardy. As the 1996 season drew near, the Jaguars and their fans were dreaming big.

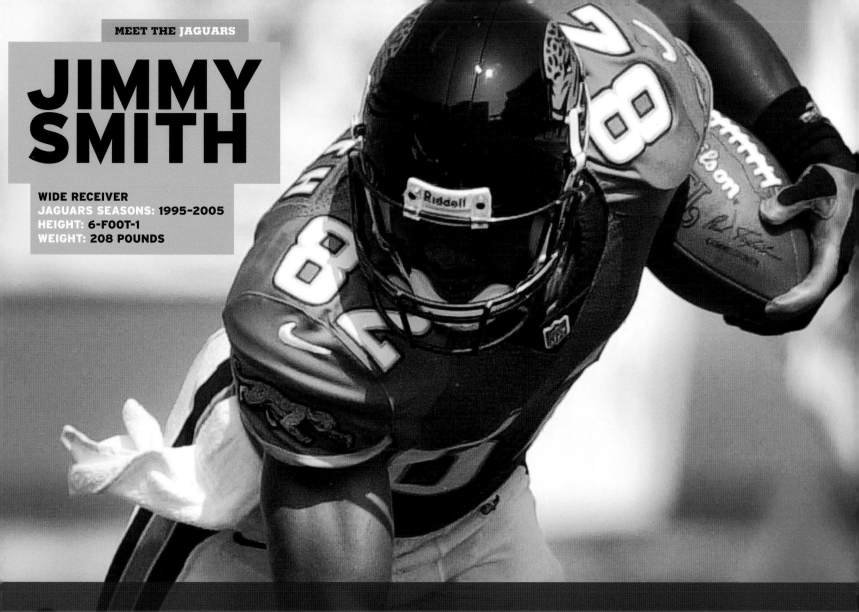

JIMMY SMITH

WIDE RECEIVER
JAGUARS SEASONS: 1995-2005
HEIGHT: 6-FOOT-1
WEIGHT: 208 POUNDS

Before arriving in Jacksonville, Jimmy Smith experienced a bumpy road in his first years as an NFL wide receiver. Coming out of Mississippi's Jackson State University, he spent two years with the Dallas Cowboys and Philadelphia Eagles before being picked up by the expansion Jaguars. By 1996, he was the most dominant receiver on the team, blowing past defenders, making spectacular grabs, and helping power the Jaguars all the way to the AFC Championship Game. One of his greatest highlights occurred in a 1998 playoff game against the New England Patriots. In the fourth quarter, with Jacksonville leading 12–10, Smith broke away from defensive back Ty Law and made a diving catch in the back of the end zone that helped Jacksonville secure the win. In 2005, after 13 NFL seasons, the five-time Pro-Bowler ended his career with 12,287 receiving yards. "We nicknamed him 'J-Smooth' because he made everything look so easy," said Baltimore Ravens cornerback Chris McAlister. "Jimmy was clearly one of the best receivers on the field. He was one of the most consistent players in the NFL, with his great combination of speed and power."

THE JAGUARS ROAR

X--------------------------------

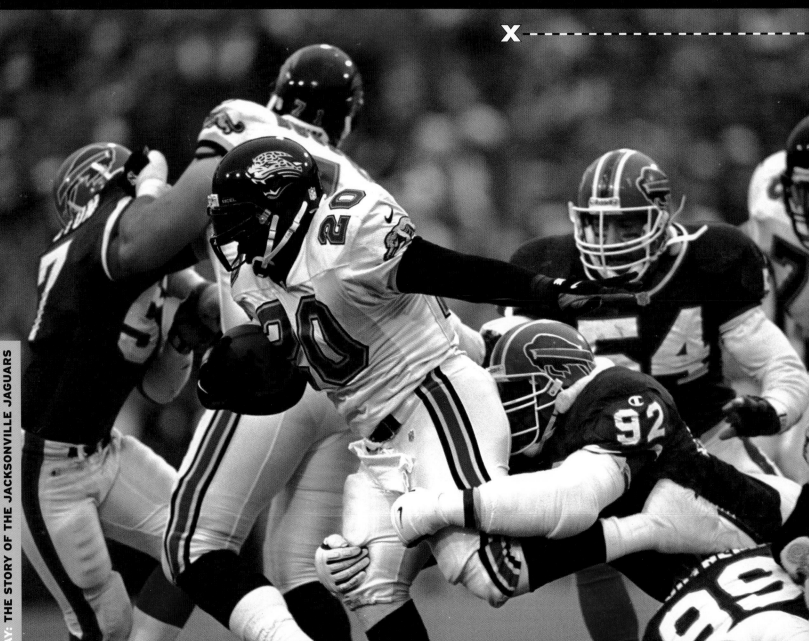

X Known for
his great power,
Natrone Means had an
unremarkable regular
season in 1996 but
was outstanding in the
playoffs, rushing for 175
and 140 yards in the first
two postseason games.

Jacksonville's second season started with a whimper, as
the team reached the midway point with a disappointing
3–5 record. But on November 24, the Jaguars topped the
Baltimore Ravens 28–25 in an overtime thriller. That game
seemed to energize the young Jaguars, who reeled off five
straight victories to end the season. Incredibly, in only its
second season, the team had put together a 9–7 record and
made the playoffs. "Everyone around the nation didn't know
who we are," said kicker Mike Hollis, whose 42-yard field goal
in the last game of the season earned the team a postseason
berth. "But they know now."

But the Jaguars weren't content to just make the
playoffs. In the first round, on the road against the Buffalo
Bills, big running back Natrone Means rumbled for 175 yards,
and Hollis banked a late fourth-quarter, 45-yard field goal
off the uprights to upset the Bills 30–27. The surprises kept
coming the next week as the Jaguars stunned the Denver
Broncos 30–27 in Denver's Mile High Stadium. In that game,
Brunell shredded the Broncos' defense with 245 passing yards.
Unbelievably, Jacksonville was just one win away from the
Super Bowl.

Although they couldn't quite complete the dream season—
losing the AFC Championship Game 20–6 to the New England

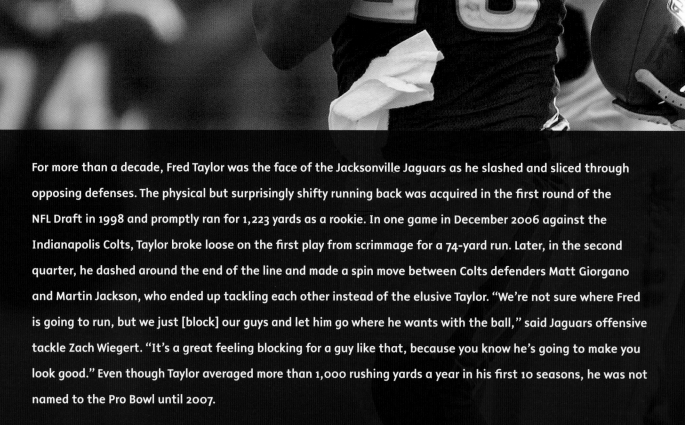

FRED TAYLOR

RUNNING BACK
JAGUARS SEASONS: 1998–2008
HEIGHT: 6-FOOT-1
WEIGHT: 230 POUNDS

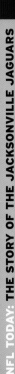

For more than a decade, Fred Taylor was the face of the Jacksonville Jaguars as he slashed and sliced through opposing defenses. The physical but surprisingly shifty running back was acquired in the first round of the NFL Draft in 1998 and promptly ran for 1,223 yards as a rookie. In one game in December 2006 against the Indianapolis Colts, Taylor broke loose on the first play from scrimmage for a 74-yard run. Later, in the second quarter, he dashed around the end of the line and made a spin move between Colts defenders Matt Giorgano and Martin Jackson, who ended up tackling each other instead of the elusive Taylor. "We're not sure where Fred is going to run, but we just [block] our guys and let him go where he wants with the ball," said Jaguars offensive tackle Zach Wiegert. "It's a great feeling blocking for a guy like that, because you know he's going to make you look good." Even though Taylor averaged more than 1,000 rushing yards a year in his first 10 seasons, he was not named to the Pro Bowl until 2007.

Patriots—the Jaguars had opened eyes around the NFL. On the season, James Stewart had teamed up with Means to post a combined 1,230 rushing yards, while speedy receiver Jimmy Smith caught 83 passes for 1,244 yards. After the Jaguars' amazing run, Coughlin was named NFL Coach of the Year.

The Jaguars began the 1997 season determined to show the world that 1996 wasn't a fluke. Although the team was dealt a serious blow when Brunell went down with a knee injury before the season, backup quarterbacks Steve Matthews and Rob Johnson stepped in to guide the team to a 3–0 start.

The Jags continued to roll after Brunell returned to the lineup. McCardell and Smith each posted more than 1,000 receiving yards on the season and, in the process, became popularly known as "Thunder and Lightning." McCardell was "Thunder" because of his willingness to run routes up the

Jimmy Smith staked a claim as one of the greatest wideouts in NFL history by assembling 7 straight seasons of at least 1,000 receiving yards.

dangerous, linebacker-patrolled middle of the field and his clutch third-down catches. Smith was "Lightning" due to his greater speed. Stewart also starred, earning a special place in Jacksonville's record books by scoring five touchdowns in a 38–21 victory over the Philadelphia Eagles. Thanks to these efforts, Jacksonville finished the year 11–5 and returned to the playoffs.

In the postseason, Jacksonville faced Denver once again. The Broncos had revenge on their minds and got it, routing the Jaguars 42–17. Despite the loss, the young Jacksonville franchise was riding high, having made the playoffs twice in three years. "It's no secret," Michael Huyghue, Jacksonville's vice president of football operations, said of the team's success. "We just had a philosophy of building with youth, with young players from the college draft and young free agents…. We thought we would try to grow the team on a three-year basis, so that the young players we had could mature to the peaks of their careers in that third year."

The Jaguars began the 1998 season 5–0, but then injuries to Brunell and Stewart threatened to derail the season. Luckily, rookie running back Fred Taylor stepped in to ignite the offense. On his very first carry, Taylor raced 52 yards for a touchdown. In another game against the Buccaneers, with

MARK BRUNELL

QUARTERBACK
JAGUARS SEASONS: 1995-2003
HEIGHT: 6-FOOT-1
WEIGHT: 217 POUNDS

In 1991, quarterback Mark Brunell led the University of Washington Huskies to a Rose Bowl victory by passing for two touchdowns and rushing for two more. He earned the game's Most Valuable Player (MVP) award for his feats on the field, but more importantly, he demonstrated his deadly versatility—a versatility he would soon unleash upon the NFL. After spending two years as a backup with the Green Bay Packers, Brunell was acquired by the Jaguars. In addition to passing for 2,168 yards in his first year as a starter, Brunell ran for 480 more, making him the second-best rusher on the team. In addition to his strong left arm and fast feet, Brunell had a reputation for being a tough player, which was showcased against the Cincinnati Bengals in a 2001 game when he smashed his fingers into the face mask of a defender. With his fingers cut and bleeding, Brunell went straight back onto the field and threw a perfect, 27-yard strike to set up the game-winning touchdown. "I didn't think he was going to go back," said receiver Jimmy Smith. "What he did, it inspired the guys. Mark makes this team go."

the Jaguars trailing 24–23 and less than three minutes to play, Taylor ran up the middle, cut back to the right, then outran Tampa Bay defenders for 70 yards to score the game-winning touchdown. "Fred gives us an added dimension we've never had before," said tight end Rich Griffith. "When he gets going, we're hard to stop." It would be a banner year for the young runner as he ended the season with 1,223 yards and 14 touchdowns.

Jacksonville's defense, meanwhile, remained one of the NFL's fiercest, thanks to end Joel Smeenge, linebacker Bryce Paup, and hard-hitting rookie safety Donovin Darius. By the end of the season, Jacksonville was 11–5 and back in the postseason. In the first round of the playoffs, Taylor tore through the Patriots' defense for 162 yards as the Jags won 25–10. A week later, however, the team fell to the New York Jets, 34–24.

Jacksonville came back hungrier than ever in 1999, soaring to a stunning 14–2 record. Along the way, the Jaguars set a franchise record by winning 11 games in a row. After a first-round playoff bye, the Jaguars looked unstoppable in round two, crushing the Miami Dolphins 62–7. For the second time in their short history, the Jaguars were just one win away from the Super Bowl. Only the Tennessee Titans—the team that

ON THE SIDELINES

BRUNELL'S BIG SCRAMBLE

On January 4, 1997, in the second round of the AFC playoffs, the Jaguars faced the mighty 13–3 Denver Broncos at Mile High Stadium, a place where Denver had not lost a playoff game in 13 years. Few people gave the second-year Jags much of a chance to win. But by halftime, Jacksonville held a slim 13–12 lead. In the third quarter, Jacksonville quarterback Mark Brunell threw a 31-yard touchdown pass to receiver Keenan McCardell, and in the fourth quarter, the Jaguars led 23–12. But quarterback John Elway and the Broncos came back, scoring a touchdown and a two-point conversion to tighten the game to 23–20. With the lead in jeopardy and Jacksonville at midfield, Brunell nearly got sacked, but he squirted away from the Denver defense. He raced right, dodged a safety, swerved left, got a block from McCardell, and scrambled all the way to Denver's 21-yard line. The highlight-reel play set up another touchdown that secured a 30–27 upset for Jacksonville. "He made huge plays all day," Elway said afterward. "You don't see a lot of guys who can make things happen like he can."

had handed the Jaguars both of their regular-season losses—stood in their way. The Titans again had their number, beating the Jags 33–14.

Despite the AFC Championship Game letdown, Jaguars owner Wayne Weaver extended Coughlin's contract through the 2003 season. "Tom Coughlin has done an outstanding job of building the Jaguars into a strong contender in the NFL," Weaver said. "The Jaguars have been very fortunate to have a leader of his skill and character."

X The Jaguars' 62–7 demolition of the Dolphins in the 1999 postseason went down in the NFL record books as the second-most lopsided playoff game ever.

PROWLING FOR
A TITLE

In 2000, the Jaguars continued to roll. In the first game of the season, they defeated the Cleveland Browns 27–7 on the road behind their Thunder and Lightning duo, which combined for almost 170 receiving yards. Although Smith and McCardell would shine all season long (each would post more than 1,200 receiving yards), and although Taylor would set a team rushing record with 1,399 yards, the Jaguars slipped to 7–9, their first losing season in five years.

The 2001 season again started well, as the Jaguars went 2–0. While Taylor missed most of the season due to injury, backup running back Stacey Mack and veteran tight end Kyle Brady helped pick up the slack. Smith also continued to cement his status as one of the league's best wide receivers. In one midseason game, he caught 15 passes for 291 yards against the Ravens, and he finished the year with more than 100 receptions. Still, the Jags went just 6–10.

Facing salary cap limitations, the Jaguars said goodbye to Tony Boselli and Seth Payne in the off-season. They also let McCardell go, breaking up the NFL's most lethal receiving

Although he would eventually suit up for five different NFL teams, tough and sure-handed wideout Keenan McCardell spent his prime years running routes in Jacksonville's Alltel Stadium. X

tandem. When the 2002 Jaguars posted another 6–10 record, team ownership decided that a change was needed at the top as well, and Coughlin was replaced as head coach by former NFL linebacker Jack Del Rio. Despite being only 39 years old, Del Rio had been defensive coordinator for the Carolina Panthers, where he took a last-place defense and turned it into one of the league's best in just one year. "We're going to put the intensity back in this stadium," Coach Del Rio promised the Jacksonville faithful.

Before the 2003 season, the Jaguars drafted Byron Leftwich, a big (6-foot-5 and 245 pounds) and confident quarterback who had been a star at Marshall University. Brunell was beginning to slow down, and the team hoped that Leftwich—along with other talented additions such as veteran defensive end Hugh Douglas and linebacker Mike Peterson—would lead the Jaguars back among the AFC's elite.

The 2003 season started badly for the Jaguars, with four straight losses. Even worse, Brunell was sidelined due to an elbow injury in the third game, forcing Leftwich into the starting lineup earlier than planned. Although shaky at first, he showed poise in the fifth game of the season against the San Diego Chargers. In the fourth quarter, with less than 3 minutes to play and the ball at the Jaguars' 10-yard line, Leftwich rolled

A BLOWOUT SEASON

The Jaguars enjoyed their best season in 1999, when the five-year-old franchise went 14–2. The record was not only the best in Jaguars history; it was also the best in the NFL that year. Jacksonville dominated teams throughout the season, but the Jaguars' most spectacular win that year occurred in the playoffs, when they blew out the Miami Dolphins 62–7. Before the game, skeptics had questioned Jacksonville's legitimacy, noting that none of its 14 wins had come against teams with winning records. Quarterback Mark Brunell silenced those critics on the opening series by engineering a 73-yard touchdown drive. On Jacksonville's third possession, halfback Fred Taylor (pictured) busted through the right end, slipped through Miami defenders, and sprinted 90 yards for a touchdown. By halftime, the score was 41–7, Jacksonville. All told, the Jaguars racked up 530 yards of offense, forced 7 Miami turnovers, and held the Dolphins to only 131 yards of offense. "It was a great day for the Jaguars," Jacksonville coach Tom Coughlin said. "I think we all understand a little bit better what home-field advantage is all about, because our stadium was rocking and rolling today."

ON THE SIDELINES

DON'T BLINK DEFENSE

Success in the NFL almost always requires a great defense. Without it, most teams don't make it very far. In 2005, the Jaguars posted a 12–4 record largely due to their defense. The defense gave up only 269 points (sixth-fewest in the NFL that year) and allowed a mere 4 rushing touchdowns. One of the secrets to their success was the defensive tackle tandem of Pro-Bowlers Marcus Stroud and John Henderson. The two were a virtual wall for opposing running backs, combining for 113 tackles. Perhaps Jacksonville's finest defensive showing that year took place in an October game against the Pittsburgh Steelers. On the Steelers' opening drive, Jaguars cornerback Terry Cousin intercepted a Tommy Maddox pass. Later, Jacksonville linebacker Mike Peterson snagged an interception of his own. In overtime, with the game tied 17–17 and the Steelers holding the ball on their own 35-yard line, Jaguars cornerback Rashean Mathis stepped in front of a Maddox pass and returned it 41 yards for the game-winning touchdown. "We've got a saying around here: 'Don't blink,' because you never know what's going to happen," Mathis said.

out and threw a pass to Taylor, who broke loose and dashed 60 yards for a touchdown, securing a 27–21 victory. Even though Brunell eventually healed, Coach Del Rio decided to stay with the rookie. Leftwich made plenty of mistakes, and the Jaguars finished a mere 5–11, but Jags fans had reason to hope as their new quarterback gained valuable experience and the Jacksonville "D" finished as the NFL's second-best run defense, allowing an average of just 87 yards a game.

During the off-season, Jacksonville traded Brunell to the Washington Redskins. The team also continued to add young

X Byron Leftwich was probably the slowest-running quarterback in the league, but few passers could match his size and strength.

talent, signing star safety Deon Grant from the Carolina Panthers and selecting wide receiver Reggie Williams with the ninth overall pick in the 2004 NFL Draft.

Leftwich led the Jaguars to a fast 3–0 start in 2004, with all of the victories coming by three points or fewer. The most dramatic win was the season's first game, at Buffalo. With time expiring, Leftwich threw a seven-yard pass to rookie wide receiver Ernest Wilford, who made a leaping catch between three Bills defenders to give the Jaguars the victory. "Good teams find a way to win, and we want to become a good team," said Del Rio, whose team had lost numerous close games the previous year.

The rest of the season was a roller-coaster ride for Jacksonville. The Jaguars captured last-minute wins against the Indianapolis Colts and Kansas City Chiefs. But they also suffered painful losses such as a late-season, 21–0 defeat at home to the Houston Texans, which knocked them out of the playoffs. Still, the team improved to 9–7, putting Jacksonville back in the hunt.

Players such as young wide receiver Ernest Wilford helped the 2004 Jaguars go 9–7 and take a step back toward contention in the AFC. X

GARRARD TAKES
THE REINS

Jacksonville flew high in 2005, thanks in part to a fleet of big passing targets that included 260-pound tight end George Wrighster (left) and 6-foot-6 receiver Matt Jones (right).

Before the start of the 2005 season, the Jaguars signed pass-rushing defensive end Reggie Hayward away from the Broncos and selected speedy, 6-foot-6 wide receiver Matt Jones in the NFL Draft. With both its defense and offense bolstered, Jacksonville was ready to make a run for the playoffs.

The Jaguars toppled the Seattle Seahawks 26–14 in their opening game of 2005, as Leftwich connected with Smith twice for touchdowns. Almost midway through the season, carrying a 4–3 record, Jacksonville took on the Texans. For the first half, the Jaguars were shut out by Houston's 31st-ranked defense. But Leftwich refused to let the game or the season get away. He completed all of his second-half passes, including a 23-yard toss to Smith to set up the game-winning touchdown. "He took responsibility for the outcome of that game," said Jaguars running back Alvin Pearman. "He really put the game on his shoulders."

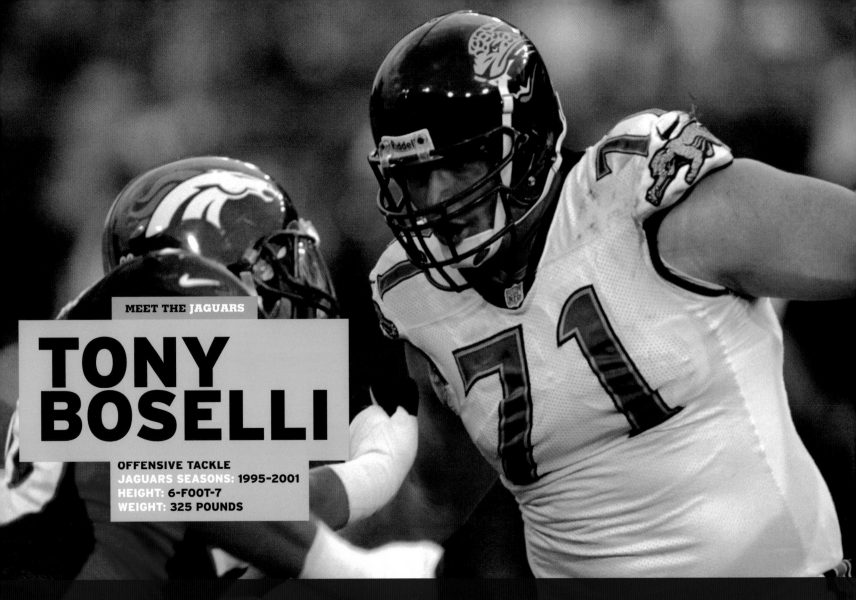

TONY BOSELLI

OFFENSIVE TACKLE
JAGUARS SEASONS: 1995-2001
HEIGHT: 6-FOOT-7
WEIGHT: 325 POUNDS

Tony Boselli was widely regarded as one of the NFL's finest offensive tackles of the 1990s. He was one of those rare offensive linemen both quick enough to excel at pass protection and strong enough to blast open holes for running backs. During his college career at the University of Southern California, Boselli was a first-team All-American in 1994 and 1995. He was the first player ever to be drafted by the Jaguars and went on to make the Pro Bowl five times. He played seven seasons for the Jaguars before being picked by the Houston Texans in the NFL's 2002 expansion draft, but injuries forced him to retire just a year later. On March 21, 2006, he signed a one-day contract with Jacksonville so he could officially retire as part of the team. Soon after, he became the first player to be inducted into the Jaguars' Ring of Honor. "It's appropriate to have Tony as the first member of the Ring of Honor as one of the all-time great Jaguars," said team owner Wayne Weaver. "Others will follow later, but Tony will be the first."

That victory got the Jaguars on a roll, and they won their next four games. But in a matchup against the Arizona Cardinals, they lost Leftwich for the rest of the season with a broken ankle. Backup quarterback David Garrard filled in and played brilliantly, leading the Jaguars the rest of the way to a 12–4 record. Leftwich returned to the starting lineup for a playoff game against the Patriots, but the Jaguars fell 28–3. In the off-season, the team suffered another loss when star wide receiver Jimmy Smith retired after 11 seasons in Jacksonville. "He was one of the great Jaguars and certainly one of the great receivers in NFL

X Although they did their best to rough up star quarterback Peyton Manning, the 2005 Jaguars lost both of their matchups with the division rival Colts.

history," said Jacksonville vice president James Harris. "Most people will say that he's one of the best pure route runners in the game, and we will all hate to see Jimmy go."

The Jaguars endured a bumpy start to the 2006 season, going 3–2 before losing Leftwich to another ankle injury in a loss to the Texans. Garrard once again found himself directing the offense and led the Jaguars to victory in five of the next seven games, including a 37–17 thumping of the Tennessee Titans. In a late-season game against Indianapolis, a new star emerged as rookie running back Maurice Jones-Drew rushed for 166 yards and returned a kickoff 93 yards for a touchdown to help the Jaguars crush the Colts 44–7. With three games left, Jacksonville stood at 8–5, poised for the playoffs. But it then lost its final three games, all of them by seven points or fewer, to finish the year a disappointing 8–8 and out of the playoffs.

Before the 2007 season, the Jaguars decided to release the injury-prone Leftwich and promote Garrard to starting quarterback full-time. Garrard made the decision look good as he passed for more than 2,500 yards and didn't throw an interception until Week 13. The defense also played its part as end Paul Spicer recorded a team-high 7.5 sacks and safety Reggie Nelson set a team rookie

HOME OF THE JAGS

In November 1993, when the NFL officially awarded Jacksonville a new franchise, the city's first order of business was to find a home for the new team. Since Gator Bowl Stadium was already 45 years old, the city decided to demolish it and built a new arena. The Jaguars and the city of Jacksonville spent $134 million, and in slightly more than 19 months, Jacksonville Municipal Stadium was completed in time for opening day in 1995. It was the first time in NFL history that an expansion team was going to play its first season in a brand-new stadium. The stadium, which could hold more than 67,000 fans, featured two 156-foot-wide scoreboards anchored at each end zone. In 1997, Alltel Communications bought a 10-year naming contract, and the field became Alltel Stadium. In 2005, it hosted Super Bowl XXXIX. For the event, the city spent an additional $47 million on improvements, including the addition of escalators in the stands above each end zone. In 2007, after Alltel's contract ended, the stadium went back to being called Jacksonville Municipal Stadium.

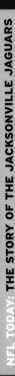
MEET THE JAGUARS

TOM COUGHLIN

COACH
JAGUARS SEASONS: 1995-2002

Tom Coughlin became head coach of the Jacksonville Jaguars on February 21, 1994. Before he joined the expansion team, he had earned a reputation as a brilliant coach at Boston College, where he turned a struggling program into a top-20 team in just 3 years. Coughlin brought his tough-as-nails coaching style to Jacksonville, where he instituted a rigid list of rules for players, such as no slouching during team meetings and kneeling during practice. Breaking any of the rules meant getting a fine. But his strict discipline paid off as he led the Jaguars to the AFC Championship Game in the team's second year. "One of his theories is that players subconsciously play at 90 to 95 percent of their level," said defensive tackle John Jurkovic. "You only do as much as you need to do to be successful. What he tries to do is push you to the max and get 100 percent out of you all the time." Coughlin was fired in 2002 after three losing seasons, and he went on to coach the New York Giants, leading them to a Super Bowl victory in 2007.

record with 5 interceptions. Thanks to these efforts and those of the short but powerful Jones-Drew, Jacksonville went 11–5 and earned a spot in the postseason as an AFC Wild Card team.

The Jaguars' offense struggled in an opening-round playoff matchup against the Pittsburgh Steelers. But the defense came up big, sacking Steelers quarterback Ben

X Quarterback David Garrard (left) and halfback Maurice Jones-Drew (right) led the way offensively as the 2007 Jaguars roared to the playoffs.

NFL TODAY: THE STORY OF THE JACKSONVILLE JAGUARS

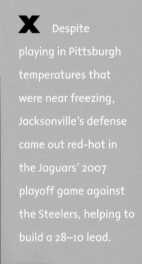

X Despite playing in Pittsburgh temperatures that were near freezing, Jacksonville's defense came out red-hot in the Jaguars' 2007 playoff game against the Steelers, helping to build a 28–10 lead.

Roethlisberger six times and intercepting three of his passes to hang on to a 31–29 victory. Unfortunately, the next week, the high-powered, 16–0 New England Patriots were too much for the Jaguars to handle. Jacksonville put up a fight but fell 31–20.

Before the 2008 season, the Jaguars rewarded Garrard's poised and steady play with a new seven-year contract. "To have David lead the team for the next seven years, it really gives us the stability and the continuity that we need to compete at the highest level and bring a championship to Jacksonville," said owner Wayne Weaver. But Garrard struggled with interceptions in 2008, and the Jaguars were plagued by a host of injuries, plummeting to the bottom of the AFC South in a season that Jacksonville fans were eager to forget. "We're the 'black cloud' Jags right now," said Taylor. "But we're going to shake that off and get a little more sunshine around here."

In just over a decade, the Jacksonville Jaguars have become one of the most remarkable success stories in NFL

X By 2008, the Jaguars had a reputation as one of the most physical teams in the NFL, putting lumps on the opposition, win or lose.

X The Jaguars had high expectations in 2008 but came out of the gate slowly, holding a 3–5 record by the midpoint of the season.

history. After making the playoffs in four of its first five seasons, the Florida franchise clawed its way to two AFC Championship Games and produced such stars as Fred Taylor and Jimmy Smith. With a little luck, the day may soon come when Jacksonville Jaguars teal and gold are the colors of world champions.

A ONE-TWO PUNCH

In 2006 and 2007, the Jaguars had one of the NFL's best one-two running attacks. During those years, veteran running back Fred Taylor and young Maurice Jones-Drew (pictured, left) combined for more than 4,000 rushing yards and 32 touchdowns. Despite an age difference of nearly a decade, the two accomplished many of the same feats. Both were the only running backs in Jacksonville history to have recorded multiple 100-yard rushing games in their rookie year, and each had a streak of eight consecutive games of scoring a touchdown. The luxury of having two terrific running backs was clearly illustrated in a 37–17 win over the Houston Texans in October 2007. In that game, the duo combined for 215 rushing yards. One play, Taylor smashed through the line and sprinted for a 76-yard gain. In another series, Jones-Drew broke two tackles, outran a defender, and then flipped head-over-heels into the end zone. "When you run the ball for nine-point-something yards a carry in this league, you're kicking somebody's tail," said Texans coach Gary Kubiak. "That was ours they were kicking."

INDEX